Castles in the Air

New and Collected Poems by

Silvia Kofler

Spartan
Press

Spartan Press

Kansas City, Missouri

 Spartan
Press

Copyright © Silvia Kofler, 2026

First Edition: 1 3 5 7 9 10 8 6 4 2

ISBN: 979-8-89975-027-4

LCCN: 2026930119

Author photo: Denise Zeikle

Cover image: Carla Nace

Acknowledgments:

"Almost Wild Mustangs" published as *Horse Poems Postcard #59* from Cross-Cultural Communications, NY, 2019

"Crossings" *Elder Leaf: An Ekphrastic Experience,* Bruce McClain, Kansas City, MO 2023, Korean Expatiate Literature #29, Tustin, CA 2025.

"Deletions" *Voices of Israel,* Volume 48, 2022

"Golden" *I-70 Review*, Summer/Fall 2021, Menzione d'Onore (Honorable Mention), International Poetry Contest, Solferini, Italy, 2024.

"One- Eyed Toyotas" Korean Expatiate Literature # 29 Tustin, CA 2025.

"Peripatetic" and "Postal" *Shabdaguchha*, an international bilingual (Bengali-English) poetry magazine, Woodhaven, NY, 2024

"Poem for Yesterday" appeared in *Rockhurst Reflects: September 11, 2001*

"Resizing America" *I-70 Review,* 2018

"Scattered" *Korean Expatriate Literature*, Tustin, CA 2023

"Street Cars" *Curating Home,* A Kansas City Poetry Anthology, Woodneath Press, 2021

"Talking Heads" co-published by *Korean Expatiate Literature* & Cross-Cultural Communications, New York 2024

"Trinkets" *Voices of Israel*, Volume 47, 2021

"Vertigo" and "Trumpet Vine" Voices of Israel, Volume 44, 2017

"Zero Sum" Bridging the Water IV, an international bilingual (Korean-English) poetry anthology, co-published by *Korean Expatiate Literature* & Cross-Cultural Communications, New York 2023 https://masticadoresusa.wordpress.com/2023/07/15/zero-sum-by-silvia-kofler/

Table of Contents

For Dave Paarmann and all my
supportive friends and publishers

*Only by the always-bodily thing are we
brought to what our brains conceive
before the body falls like a tree.*

-Philip Miller

Castles in the Air

Crossings

After an image by Bruce McClain

The gnarled head looms
large against the railroad tracks
resting on the forefinger of
the hand on the other side
of vanishing tracks
ponders the arrival at the crossroads
embraces the leaves of nature.

Staring straight ahead
with tightly closed lips
a mind exposed
to buildings left behind
nearing the end of the journey
to the other side
of vanishing tracks.

Green Monkeys

After "Green Monkeys" by Dave Paarmann

Green monkeys
jump in caged squares
of dark matter
of a space wave
universe
of signals lost in
curves and crannies
of white space
dotted with red splatters
of golden globe
where shadowy humans
are scattered in a
chaotic mosaic
inhabited by solitary age defying
shorts clad jogger

sprinting toward
the inevitable sunless curves
of gravity.

Castles in the Air

Thoughts drift as
I cuddle barely awake
against a mountain of pillows,
not ready to face a new day
of goals to reach
in the reality of daylight.

September 11, 1973
Palacio de La Moneda tumbles
democracy falls
by la moneda de USA.

September 11, 2001 the towers fall
in New York.
Were the terrorists aware
of parallel dates?
I wonder as I build my
castles in the air.

Boarding

The young man's head with
red, black and white dyed hair
looks like a moving flag
as he practices his jumps
and swooshes along the concrete railings
outside Poets House's Elizabeth Kray Hall.
My mind wanders after listening for hours to
readings from an English and Korean anthology.
When will it be my turn to read my poems?
When will I hear them in Korean?
I long to be outside in the sunlight
of Battery Park,
jumping and swooshing on my skateboard

savoring the poetry
of youth.

Camping

Camping is the *de rigueur du jour*.
RVs have become a hot commodity as
we yearn to travel freely.
Social distancing
becomes a complicated travel fun-killer
when smiles are invisible behind masked faces.
Camping and escaping into nature
makes distancing
from those not in our bubble easier.
We can pretend everything is normal
as we observe wildlife
and swim in the lake.
But, we haven't forgotten
the mosquitos
and damp nights in tents.
We sip wine and dine al fresco
in our backyard,
the nightly visits by raccoons
and opossums
wildlife enough for now.

Scattered

Friends appear on the
Facebook page as random distractions
during my stay in Telluride, Colorado.
John appears to be in Cartagena, Colombia
for a sail boat race. It must be quite the race
because he even notices a motorcade with
Iván Duque Márquez, its current president.
Tammy is on her way to an Oahu,
Honolulu adventure,
she posts from an overlook path
with an ocean background
that reminds me of my visit years ago.
Susan is in Tampa, Florida
lounging on her favorite beach.
The grand prize goes to
a couple of neighbors,
who are in Antarctica
for a marathon.

Still, post pandemic shutdowns
I long to meet up at our corner bar.

Degrees of Fame Separation

Six degrees of separation is the idea that all people on average are six, or fewer, social connections away from each other.

I used to swim in Thalersee
where Arnold Schwarzenegger
proposed to Maria Schriver.
Neighbors knew his mother.

I used to live in Garches
west of Paris.
I was an Au Pair who conversed
and taught German to the daughters.
Monsieur Sabouret
was a French General
and enjoyed talking to me in English.
One evening he told me about Indochina,
the French knew to pull out of Vietnam.
He was in his dress uniform and
complained that he had to attend
a state dinner. He was not thrilled about it.
Only years later, it dawned on me
that he had dinner
with president Valéry Giscard d'Estaing.

I used to attend many readings
before the pandemic
and had dinner with Richard Blanco
who told me to visit

if I am in the area of Bethel Maine.
He was the inaugural poet for
Barack Obama in January 2009.

The idea of six degrees of separation
seems to be true.

Trinkets

The silver curlicue
earrings are ribbons flowing
from her earlobes.
Every day she wears them
compliments abound and she
explains that she bought them in Trondheim, Norway.
It is not the frivolous purchase of the trinket
that brings her joy,
but the memory of a trip to a city her
father used to tell stories about.
She remembers climbing the
steep spiral staircase
to the top of Nidaros' cathedral
with her smiling friends
looking at the fjord
wondering if he climbed those stairs
during World War II.

Star Wars Opera

Listening to the piano player
accompany the soprano
as she performs "I Love Paris"
during the opera open mike
while I stare at the muted
close captioned television screen
behind Californos bar in Westport
and watch Han Solo fight
enemy forces in
Solo: A Star Wars Story
creates a dissonance
as I recall
Luke Skywalker searching
for Lea as he fights
against the dark forces
swinging his light saber
on a screen in Paris
where I saw Star Wars
in a theatre on the Champs-Elysées
reaching for the stars.

Deletions

We can remove monuments
and statues of painful symbols,
change street names,
change names of sports teams
delete the logos and names
of popular brands.
Pol Pot tried to create a utopian agrarian
society and declared *This is Year Zero*
to erase the history of Cambodia in 1975;
25 percent of the population
perished during his rule.
After the Russian Revolution the city of
St. Peterburg became Leningrad in 1924,
but the name was not forgotten,
after the collapse of the Soviet Union
Leningrad voters chose to reclaim
its former name in 1991 and
original names of many streets
and bridges returned.
Amending the past
is a tricky business.

Vertigo

Glancing at one's feet
standing on a Plexiglas ledge
103 stories above ground
puts existence
in a comical
juxtaposition of
illusory support,
support that may give way to
trembling quakes
of tectonic shifts.

Golden

My brother spray-painted his
WC gold and called it his throne.
I still remember his second-floor apartment
at Schillerstrasse
where he gave elaborate parties
and I spent one New Year's Eve
bash on a trip home from Paris
where I lived for three years.
He had moved out of my parents' apartment
when I was eight years old and
we shared little time together
throughout the years.
Looking at one of his small
still life paintings
and a drawing of me
sitting with an open book in my hands,
I remember the few golden moments
we spent before his death
at age thirty-three.

New Year's Strings

Strings tangle in front
of my eyes
as I proffer
the open box of poppers to
a friend who leaves early
to make it to
one more party.

He reaches into the box
grabs a handful and remarks:
*They look just like
colorful tampons.*

A few days later,
I tell a friend. He chuckles:
*It could make for an
explosive confusion.*

Resizing America

There was no size zero, let alone the triple zeroes that sometimes are in stores today. As American girth increased, so did egos. And thus began the practice of vanity sizing.

-Laura Stampler in *Time*

She didn't notice it
right away,
it was a gradual decline,
a sliding
down the
playground's plastic
curved incline.
It was like looking in the mirror
and noticing slight differences,
a wrinkle here
a sagging breast there.

Over a number of years she denied
the evidence.
It couldn't be that she
shrank that much,
or could it be?
A decline in height
for humans is
evidence of aging
unlike a tree's
increase in height over
the years.
But did she really

shrink in girth from a size five
to a size zero?
Lately, she even noticed that she could fit
into a double-zero dress.

It must be true,
she is shrinking,
numbers don't lie.

Button Snob

He meanders through the aisles
touches a number of shirts
and examines a pair of trousers
till he discovers
a shirt that appeals
to him for its texture and the right cut.
This is a great color for you
buy it, I encourage him
after getting bored
cruising the aisles.
He seems to agree,
but before he decides to buy it
the buttons have to be counted,
because no shirt short of seven buttons
will be considered.
I wonder what made him follow
this button-count rule
and smile at his persnickety ways.

Talking Heads

Talking heads swirl
around my brain like
water flowing
down my shower drain.
Even if I try to tune them out
they appear ubiquitous.
Experts spouting probabilities
polls of endless data heaps
causing my perplexion.

Robo-call hang-ups,
missed calls congregations,
a cackling gaggle of geese
on my cell's missed call logs.
Call backs futile answers:
the number is no longer
available, or may be out of service.

The only Talking Heads
I hear swim
in rushing eddies and
sing about
wild wild life
and *take me down*
to the river.

Zero Sum

The worst thing about a zero sum game is that the minute someone begins to play one, it puts you in a lose-lose situation. If you don't fight for your own best interest, you lose. If you do, you're now in a war where both of you will get hurt even if you are the one who wins. Integration is the end of the zero sum game.

The game of Chess
has two opponents trying
to capture the opposing leader
and rule the land,
the game of Go uses stones
to form territories
by surrounding vacant
areas on the board.
The Russian despot adapted his plan
to the ancient game of Go
to pursue his dream of capturing territories
lost 33 years ago for Russian speakers
of an integrated Ukraine
to capture ports of power.

The endgame's fallen bones
speak no language.

Doodles

The puffy fellow
runs along the sidewalk
and smiles at us
from the cosmos comic page.

We select the doodles
of life's given choices:
Puffy jolly guy
strolling with friends,
nervous gal
teetering along the
sidewalk on six-inch heels
on a lonely sidewalk,
hampered
never running along the
free space
of a self-created path.

Signs

The sidewalks are empty
as I stroll along the boulevard,
during the waning daylight
I watch my surroundings
I am alone.
People advise me that if you notice
a car slowing its speed
walk, or run, into the opposite direction.
I notice illuminated signs
and their flaws
that usually escape my notice.
The "S" for SUNFRESH
remains dark, the remaining
"UNFRESH" for the supermarket
elicits a chuckle.
CHILDREN'S MERCY
misses the ME
reads "CHILDREN'S RCY"
I won't notice the missing letters
when I drive along the boulevard.

Peripatetic

Our toes hurt
because she moves to
some loud rock beat.

Years ago she made
us pose in St. Cast Brittany,
at France's North coast
to draw us
in pencil strokes.

Three decades later
she posed us to paint
us for an other portrait
in Kansas City, Missouri.

Who knows,
maybe she will want to
pose us for a sculpture
next time.

Who knows
where that may be.

Does she think she can abuse us
just like years ago.
We may just go on strike
and refuse to move her.

Postal

Slapping the self-stick stamps
onto fifty envelopes suggests
just how terrible it must be
to perform
one task over and over...

I dawdle to
observe other customers
in the self-service lobby at the post office,
delight at the observation that just about
every other individual double-checks the mail slot
(I tend to double-check)
after dropping mail,
just to make sure.

Just to make sure.
Forced to double-check
every day
for eight hours
may turn any worker
postal.

Mozart Men

They are on every main street corner
of downtown Vienna.
Especially in the close vicinity
of the Opera house.
Clad in bright red and gold
embroidered cloaks they peddle
classical music events
like the market hucksters
of earlier days.
We wait for my friend
and I text her:
*You can find us by the Mozart Man and his stand
in front of the Albertina museum*

milking music masters.

Trumpet Vine

My neighbor hates its invasiveness
and lopped off as much as
she could on her side of the fence.
However, birds love it and
sparrows moved into the birdhouse
beneath its canopy.
Hummingbirds flock to its fiery
orange blooms in July.

I remember the trumpet vines
climbing up the railing
next to father's balcony swing
at his home in Austria.
I noticed their beauty
and he announced:
You should recognize it
it is an American plant.

Sorting through
old photographs
I look at his image on the balcony
of the house I sold after his death
and love the vine even more.

Street Cars

There once was one called *Desire*
Kansas City enjoyed them
fifty years ago
until Detroit carmakers
made them disappear.
Some tracks are still
left over in old Westport.
Now, we've got a new line,
all 2.2 miles of it.
Its streetcars are sleeker
and quieter than fifty years ago.
However, some car accustomed drivers
haven't learned to park
within the white lines
and a Benz took a beating.
A lady stopped on its
tracks motions the conductor to
drive around her car.
After fifty years it takes some
getting used to.

The Powers to Be

I remember the adage
Be careful what you wish for,
it might just come true.

The gods of AI and
social media, a typhoon,
swept through the country
to destroy all
obstructing their path.

The gods of power
won, but don't count
on the gods to care about
your house.

Almost Wild Mustangs

Herds of wild horses,
descendants of the horses
brought across the Atlantic
by Spanish conquistadors centuries ago,
gallop through the Flint Hills of Kansas.
By the 20th century the horses
were pushed into federal lands
of Western states.
Protected by the Wild Free-Roaming-Horse
and Burro Act of 1971
they are not so wild
as they roam the grasslands.
Ranchers submit bids to
the Bureau of Land Management
to take care of them.
The barely wild mustangs are a
a mix of palominos,
pintos, and whites
crowding around a farmer's pickup
as he delivers bales of hay
during the cold months.

They remind me of their origins
on a different continent,
where I have seen the stud farm
of the Lipizzaner horses
whose coats turn pale like snow

at the age of ten to be sent
to the Spanish Riding School in Vienna
to lose any semblance of their wild origins.

One-Eyed-Toyotas

One-Eyed-Toyotas
stick to my neurons
like flies to flypaper,
the kind that used to hang from light-
fixtures before screened in windows
and central air.

We drive to our friends' house to watch football,
even though I barely know the rules,
but we enjoy the company
and the outbursts of
serious football fans,
and you exclaim
Look, a One–Eyed-Toyota!
as you point at its single headlight.

Gathered around the TV screen
an enthusiastic older guest
jumps up from the sofa
and screams at the referee
for a reason I must have missed
and his partial flies
from his mouth and lands on the
hardwood floor next to one of the resident dogs.
He quickly grabs it off the floor and
puts it back into his mouth
without rinsing it first

as I stare bemused,
and our friend smiles and mentions:
We clean our floors every other week,
whether they need it, or not.

On our drive home
I decide that the world is full of
One-Eyed-Toyotas.

Gulfs

At the port of Antigua
sand forms fluffy eddies
of beige around the ship's bow

Walking along the beach
waves massage my feet
as I dig my toes into the sand

The Freedom of the Seas sails
along tumultuous seas
signals the gulf between North
and South America
creating waves.

Happy Hour at the Mix

Strolling along L Street in
California's capital city
we come across an inviting place
with two bars and an outside patio.
It is early and the place is still mostly empty,
it takes some time
to decide what corner to settle in.

First is the long main area bar with its
inviting glass case backdrop,
then there are the inviting seats
on the patio with chartreuse and blue pillows
against gray chairs,
but it is hot outside,
however, I like the smaller inside bar
facing the patio and finally,
after sitting down in the main room with
cushy large chairs next to the main bar first,
decide to settle in the far corner
of the bar facing the patio
with a porthole-like round window at its end
overlooking the Capital Building.

We are on vacation and linger a while
drinking wine and nibbling on small plates
of cheese and bread.

As we are ready to leave the cozy corner and its
comfortable seating
the female bartender asks us where we are from
and I reply Kansas City,
but I do not sound Midwestern enough,
I tell her that I am originally from Graz, Austria,
Arnold Schwarzenegger's home town.
She smiles and tells me to look up
at the exhaust fan in the ceiling:
We had to install it when Arnold was the Governator
because he always sat in this same leather chair you
settled in, and he always smoked cigars.

He must have liked being able to look at the Capital
Building
through that porthole window.

Gray

Sleepless jetlagged nights
fill my brain
with thoughts of travels
of the past after a last
adventure in Japan.

People I knew
have gone missing
some have probably died,
others simply forgot to make a call,
send a letter, or an email.

Found Wisdom

Adapted from titles of
the Communiversity Catalogue #173 at UMKC

Self-Healing
and the hidden potential of
therapeutic gemstones
is appealing,
I like jewelry and the
way it glitters.

Manifestation through time travel
a course in miracles.
I wish I could travel back twenty years
and know what I have learned since then,
but that would be an impossible miracle.

Ask a medium
communicating with loved ones
on the other side.
What other side exactly?
I want to know.

Mysteries of the Bee Priestess
and the idea of a matriarchal
nature spirit
appeals to me.

Naturism/Nudism 101
No last names here.
It's best to keep one's
wisdom hidden.

Idiocracy

Queuing outside the MusicBar for a performance
patrons wait to receive wristbands
to enter the establishment
to ensure they are of legal drinking age.
It is important that venues
ensure this to keep licenses.
However, why would they need to check IDs
of patrons who are obviously old enough?
Are they really taking a chance,
if they look at individuals who are
in their 50s and 60s?
It is a sign of a lack
of critical thinking ability,
or ignorance of the management,
because the guy at the door is only doing
what he is told,
even though he could display some
individual initiative,
but he probably isn't paid enough
to exert such efforts.

I am only doing what I am told
is the common refrain
from those who lack incentives
for imaginative thoughts,
a lack encouraged by the elite
of an idiocracy who desires
an easy to control unimaginative populace.

Yoga Ladies

No smiles here,
rushing and pushing passed me
in the locker room
to make it to the session on time
with their mats tucked under their arms,
relaxation and stretching is serious business.
I obviously have no clue about it
as I leisurely put on some make-up
after my time in the pool.
I thought exercise was supposed to relax,
invigorate as one follows
one's own schedule.

Poem for Yesterday

After 9-11-2001

That morning, she drives to Lawrence Kansas
to lecture at KU,
listens to NPR:
We interrupt this program….

She recalls:
In the movie
The Day After
Jason Robards sees the red glow
burned faces
while he drives to Lawrence
to lecture at KU.

She sees blue sky and lush fields,
but
the glow of vanished faces
reaches into the sky.

Climate Control

The days glide by in long quiet whispers
as the generic walls of the hotel suite engulf us.
Hotel meal choices become too familiar,
we debate dinner outings
to escape the sameness of the central air-conditioned
room where blackout blinds belie summer's heat.
Heat greets us as we leave the building.
The car parked in the glaring sun, an oven,
the steering wheel burning finger tips
as I start up the AC
to escape climate change.

The Other Side

At a certain age
we wonder about the other side.

We create paradise or hell on this side:
a haven of lush lawns and mansions with pools
for the lucky minority,
hovels for the poor majority,
or something in between.
It is the luck of the draw.
The poor hope for paradise after reaching the other side.
All I know
there is no way to know.
My guess is on eternal unconsciousness.
Then who knows,
I may end up with egg on my face
and the martyr with virgins.

Silvia Kofler is a widely published poet, translator, and educator who has read her work in many places like the Yale Club and Poets House in New York City, and at Schokoladen in Berlin, Germany. Her book *Gambol the World: Eine Weltanschauung*, by Spartan Press has been translated into Portuguese by Carlos Ramos and was published by Ghost Editions in Portugal. Currently, a small collection of her poems is being translated into Armenian by Hrant Alexanyan to be published at https://vogi-nairi.am/en/

This project was made possible, in part, by generous support from the Osage Arts Community.

Osage Arts Community provides temporary time, space and support for the creation of new artistic works in a retreat format, serving creative people of all kinds — visual artists, composers, poets, fiction and nonfiction writers. Located on a 152-acre farm in an isolated rural mountainside setting in Central Missouri and bordered by ¾ of a mile of the Gasconade River, OAC provides residencies to those working alone, as well as welcoming collaborative teams, offering living space and workspace in a country environment to emerging and mid-career artists. For more information, visit us at www.osageac.org

Osage Arts Community